Sunshine

Activity Book 3

Erarbeitet von
Stefanie Aschkar (Konstanz)
Tanja Beattie (Ebersberg)
Nadine Kerler (Ulm)
Caroline Schröder (München)

Auf der Grundlage der Ausgabe von
Birgit Hollbrügge
und Ulrike Kraaz

 Deine interaktiven Gratis-Übungen findest du hier:

1. Gehe auf scook.de.
2. Gib den unten stehenden Zugangscode in die Box ein.
3. Hab viel Spaß mit deinen Gratis-Übungen.

Dein Zugangscode auf
www.scook.de | vuyh8-2o6hh

Cornelsen

Contents

Getting started

 1 Write your name.

 2 Draw yourself.

Good morning, Mr Mole.
My name is
_____

Good morning.
My name is Mr Mole.
What's your name?

> **❗ Note**
>
> 🇬🇧   🇩🇪
>
> **p**opcorn   –   **P**opcorn
> **s**kateboard – **S**kateboard

 3 Write or draw English words you know.

123 🖊 **1** Write the numbers 1–12.

🖊⭐ Write the words.

| one | 1 | | nine | | | six | | | four | |

| seven | | | ten | |

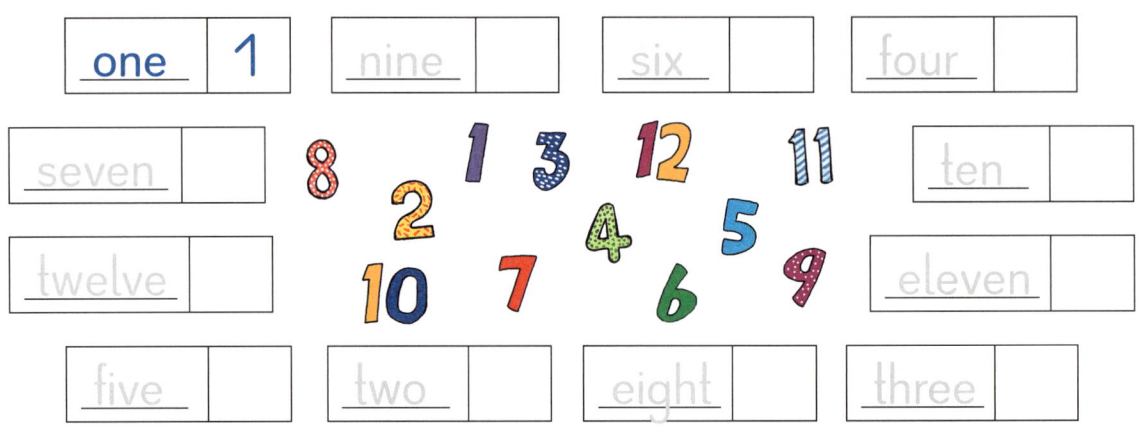

| twelve | | | eleven | |

| five | | | two | | | eight | | | three | |

🖊 **2** What do the children say? Write.

🖊 **3** How are you? Write your answer.

> I'm fine, thanks.
> I'm okay.
> I'm not very well.

Meeting friends

 1 Listen and number.

 2 Read the words.

 3 Write the words.

Note

I've got
= I have got

~~bike~~ · mountain bike · scooter · skateboard

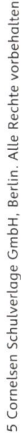

Hi. My name is Emily. I've got a <u>bike.</u>

Hi. My name is Samir. I've got a ___

Hi. My name is Kate. I've got a ___

Hi. My name is Harry. I've got a ___

1

⭐ What have you got? Talk to a partner. Write or draw.

I've got ___

I've got in-line skates. What have you got?

1 Listen. Write the phone numbers.

2 Whose number is it? Draw lines.

3 Write the names.

4 Write the names and phone numbers of your friends.

5 Listen to your teacher. Whose number is it?

⭐ Write your phone number. Talk to a partner.

My phone number is
_____

name	phone number
Paul	844589

What's your phone number?

1 Listen. Write the house numbers.

 2 Colour the doors.

blue · green · red · yellow

 3 Write the words. Check with your partner.

 Talk about the doors.

The door is _____

The door is _____

The door is _____

The door is

_____

 **4** Listen to your partner. Colour the numbers.

Please colour number 7…

Please colour number 12…

Write.

Number _____ is _____

 1 Listen to the rhyme.

 2 Read the words. Write.

 ⭐ Act out the rhyme.

Note

😀 = she   😀 = he

| brother · father · mother · sister |

This is my _____

He is very tall.

This is my _____

He is very small.

This is my _____

She likes tea.

This is my _____

She likes me.

 3 Look at the pictures. Talk about the families.

4 Listen. Whose family is it? Number the pictures.

①

②

③

 ☐

 ☐

 ☐

✏ **1** **What's your name?**

My name is _____

✏ **2** **What are your friend's names?**

My friend's names are _____

✏ **3** **How old are you?**

I'm _____

I'm three. How old are you?

✏ **4** **What's your phone number?**

My phone number is _____

✏ **5** **This is my family:**

This is my family.

✏ **6** **What's your favourite colour?**

My favourite colour is _____

| orange | blue | pink |
| green | yellow |

My favourite colour is red.

Ich fand die Aufgabe:

1 Ich kenne die vier Lehrwerkskinder. ☐   ◯ ◯ ◯

_____   _____   _____   _____

🎵14 **2** ☐ ☐ ☐ ☐ ☐ ☐ ☐ ☐ ☐ ☐   ◯ ◯ ◯

Ich habe _____ Zahlen verstanden

und aufgeschrieben. ☐

3 Ich habe zwei Kinder nach ihren   ◯ ◯ ◯

Telefonnummern gefragt. ☐

4 Ich habe mit _____   ◯ ◯ ◯
(Name)

ein Farbdiktat durchgeführt. ☐

Ich habe geprüft, ob ich die Farbwörter richtig

geschrieben habe. ☐

1 _____   2 _____   3 _____

4 _____   5 _____   6 _____

5 Ich habe _____ meine Familie   ◯ ◯ ◯
(Name)

vorgestellt. ☐

Das möchte ich noch besser können:

_____

Pets in the garden

 **1** Read and number the words.

Talk to a partner. Say: *Number one is the ...*

| | cat | | dog | | fish | | guinea pig |
| | hamster | | mouse | | rabbit | | rat |

2 Listen and write.

Talk about the pets. What colour are they?
What pet does Harry want?

What colour is the cat?

It's ...

Harry has got a _____
and a _____

Samir has got a _____

Emily has got a _____

Kate has got a _____

1 Read the words in the box.

2 Look at the pictures.
Number the words in the box.

3 Write the words.

> **! Note**
>
> = apple
>
> = apple**s**

	apple		bread		carrot		cat		dog
	fish		guinea pig		hamster		lettuce		mouse
	peanuts		rabbit		rat		tomato		

Solution: ⬜⬜⬜⬜⬜⬜⬜
1 2 3 4 5 6 7

⭐ What do you like? Talk to a partner.
Make a list.

I like worms.

✏ **1** Roll the dice. Draw lines. Work with a partner.

💬 **2** Say your sentence.

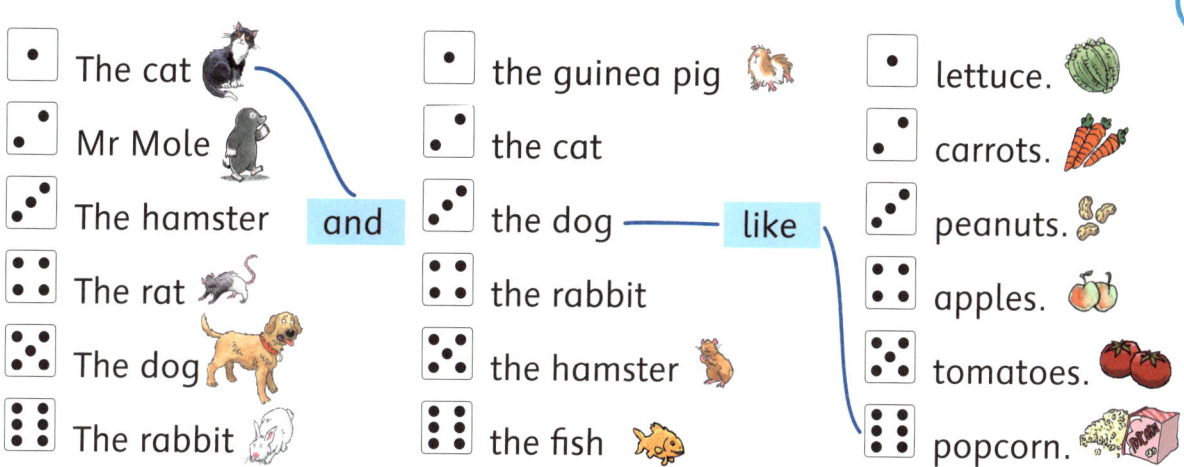

⚀ The cat		⚀ the guinea pig		⚀ lettuce.	
⚁ Mr Mole		⚁ the cat		⚁ carrots.	
⚂ The hamster	**and**	⚂ the dog	**like**	⚂ peanuts.	
⚃ The rat		⚃ the rabbit		⚃ apples.	
⚄ The dog		⚄ the hamster		⚄ tomatoes.	
⚅ The rabbit		⚅ the fish		⚅ popcorn.	

✏ **3** Roll the dice. Write the sentences.

✏ ⭐ Draw pictures.

⚀ ⚂ ⚅ The cat and the dog like popcorn.

☐ ☐ ☐ The _____ and _____ like

_____

☐ ☐ ☐ The _____ and _____ like

_____

21 **1** Listen. Number the pets. Check with a partner.

2 Tick the right food. (✓)

3 Name the pets. Write.

4 Complete the speech bubbles.

⭐ Which pets are not at the party? Circle the words in the box.

apples · carrots · fish · guinea pig · hamster
lettuce · mouse · peanuts · rabbit · rat

Portfolio: **My pets**

1 What pets do you like?

I like _____

_____

I like rabbits.

I like moles.

2 Have you got a pet? Tick. (✓)

Yes, I have. ☐   No, I haven't. ☐

! Note

I haven't = I have not

3 Write about your favourite pet.

My favourite pet is _____

My favourite pet's name is _____

It likes _____

What colour is your pet? It's _____

This is a picture of my favourite pet:

Check your English

Ich fand die Aufgabe:

leicht mittel schwer

1 Ich habe mit der Klasse den Rap

I want a dog, Mum! gesungen. ☐

◯ ◯ ◯

2 Ich habe mich mit _____
(Name)

am Telefon verabredet. ☐

◯ ◯ ◯

3 Ich habe gesagt, wie diese Tiere heißen und

sie beschriftet. ☐

◯ ◯ ◯

_____   _____   _____

_____   _____   _____

_____   _____

4 Ich habe _____ etwas über
(Name)

mein (Lieblings-) Haustier erzählt. ☐

◯ ◯ ◯

5 Ich kann diese Wörter zum Thema *food* schreiben:

◯ ◯ ◯

_____   _____   _____

_____   _____   _____

Das möchte ich noch besser können:

_____

At school

❗ Note

Can you say the word *school bag?*
Check with your teacher.

🔴 **1** Listen. Number the pictures.

👂 **2** Listen to your partner. Colour the school things.

My school things	My partner's school things

Colour the
school bag ...

Colour the
school bag ...

My pencil
is yellow.
What colour is
your pencil?

It's ...

3

 1 What can you see in the picture? Write.

⭐ Talk about the school things and the colours.

books · felt tips · glue sticks · lunch boxes · pencil cases · pencil sharpeners · pencils · pens · rubbers · rulers · ~~school bags~~ · scissors

I can see 2 school bags,

_____ rubbers,

_____

_____

_____

_____

_____

_____

_____

_____

2 Where is Mr Mole? Write.

behind · in · in front of · next to · on · under

 Mr Mole is _____ the pencil sharpener.

Mr Mole is _____ the rubber.

Mr Mole is _____ the ruler.

Mr Mole is _____ the book.

 Mr Mole is _____ the school bag.

Mr Mole is _____ the pencil case.

1 What has Kate got? Listen. Tick or cross the box. (✓) (✗)

Here you are. ✓ ✗

Sorry, I haven't got …

2 What are the children saying? Write.

⭐ Talk to a partner.

> Can I have …, please?
> Here you are.
> Sorry, I haven't got a …
> Thanks.

1 Can I have your **rubber**, please?

Yes, you can. Here you are.

Thanks.

You're welcome.

2 _____ your _____, please?

Sorry, I haven't got a **ruler**.

3 _____ your **glue stick**, _____ ?

_____

4 _____ your **scissors**, _____ ?

Yes, you can.

You're welcome.

1 Read the sentences.

colour · draw · listen · ~~read~~ · talk · write

2 Number the pictures. Write the words.

⭐ Find more words. Talk to a partner. (Look at page 18.)

① Please, read the text in the book.

② Please, _____ a lunch box.

③ Please, _____ your name.

④ Please, _____ the lunch box red.

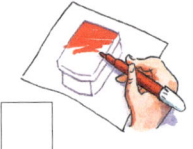

⑤ Please, _____ to your partner.

⑥ Please, _____ to your teacher.

1

3 Listen. Number the pictures.

4 What is Jack saying? Write.

Oh, dear. I haven't got…

book · pencil · red felt tip

Colour the apple red!

_____
_____
_____

Read the text!

Oh, dear. I haven't got _____

I haven't got a _____

Draw an apple!

1 Draw your school things.

 **2** Write the words. (Look at page 18.)

⭐ Present your school bag or your pencil case.

This is my school bag:

In my school bag,

there is _____

_____

_____

there are _____

_____

_____

This is my pencil case:

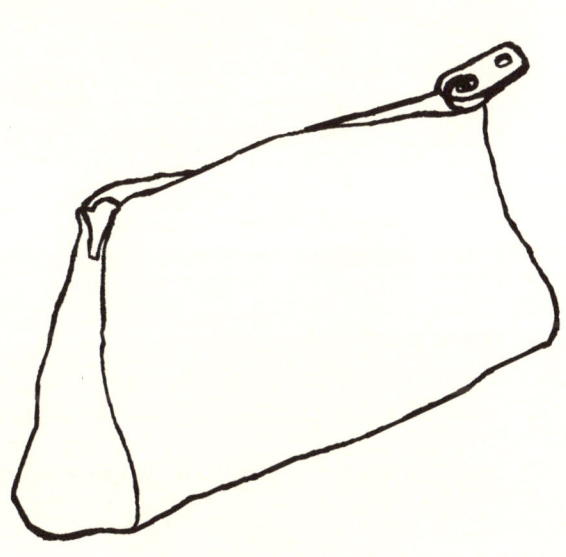

In my pencil case,

there is _____

_____

_____

there are _____

_____

_____

© 2015 Cornelsen Schulverlage GmbH, Berlin. Alle Rechte vorbehalten.

twenty-one **21**

Check your English

Ich fand die Aufgabe:

leicht mittel schwer

○ ○ ○

1 Ich habe mit der Klasse das Lied

My school things gesungen. ☐

31

2

☐ ☐ ☐ ☐ ☐ ☐ ☐ ☐

○ ○ ○

Ich habe _____ Gegenstände richtig nummeriert. ☐

3 Ich habe _____ gesagt,
                     (Name)

welche der oben abgebildeten Dinge ich in meiner

Federmappe habe und welche nicht. ☐

○ ○ ○

4

○ ○ ○

Ich habe mit _____ ein Farbdiktat
                        (Name)

durchgeführt. ☐

Das möchte ich noch besser können:

_____

The second-hand shop

1 Listen. Colour the clothes.

⭐ What's Mr Mole wearing? Talk to a partner.

2 Say the words. Draw or write what comes next.

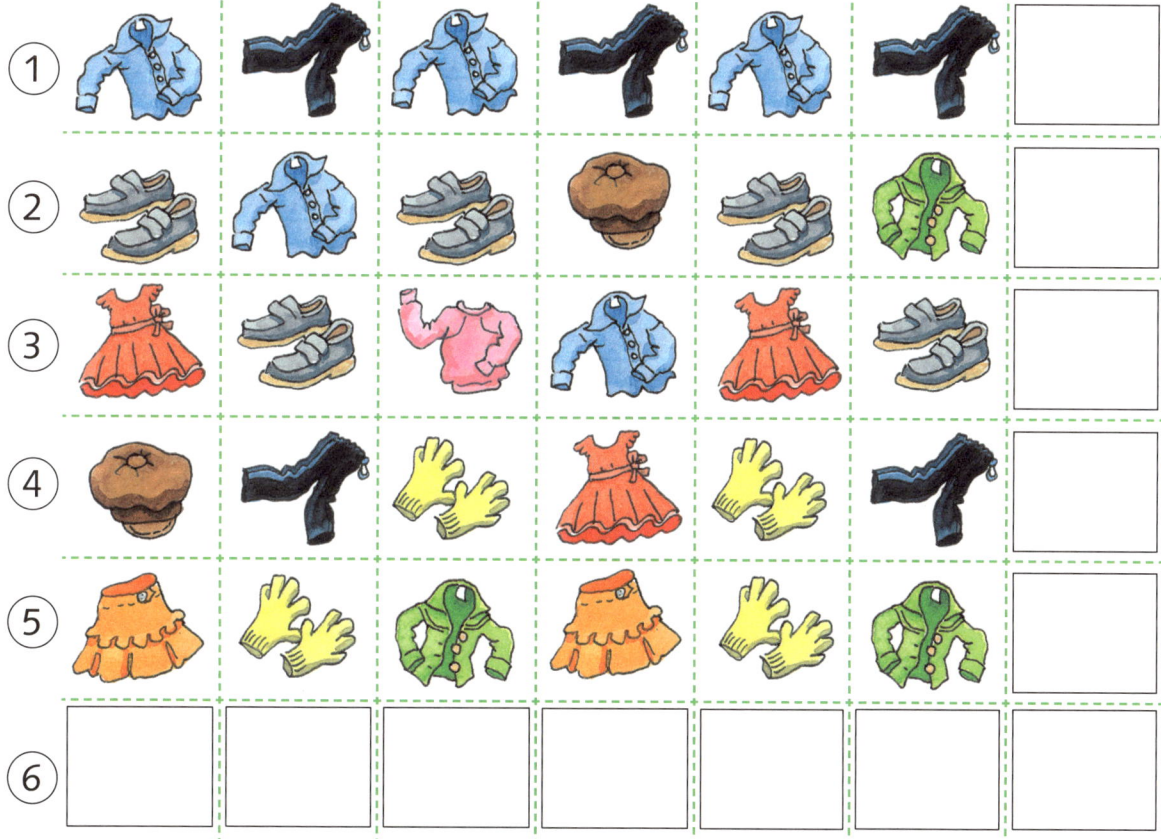

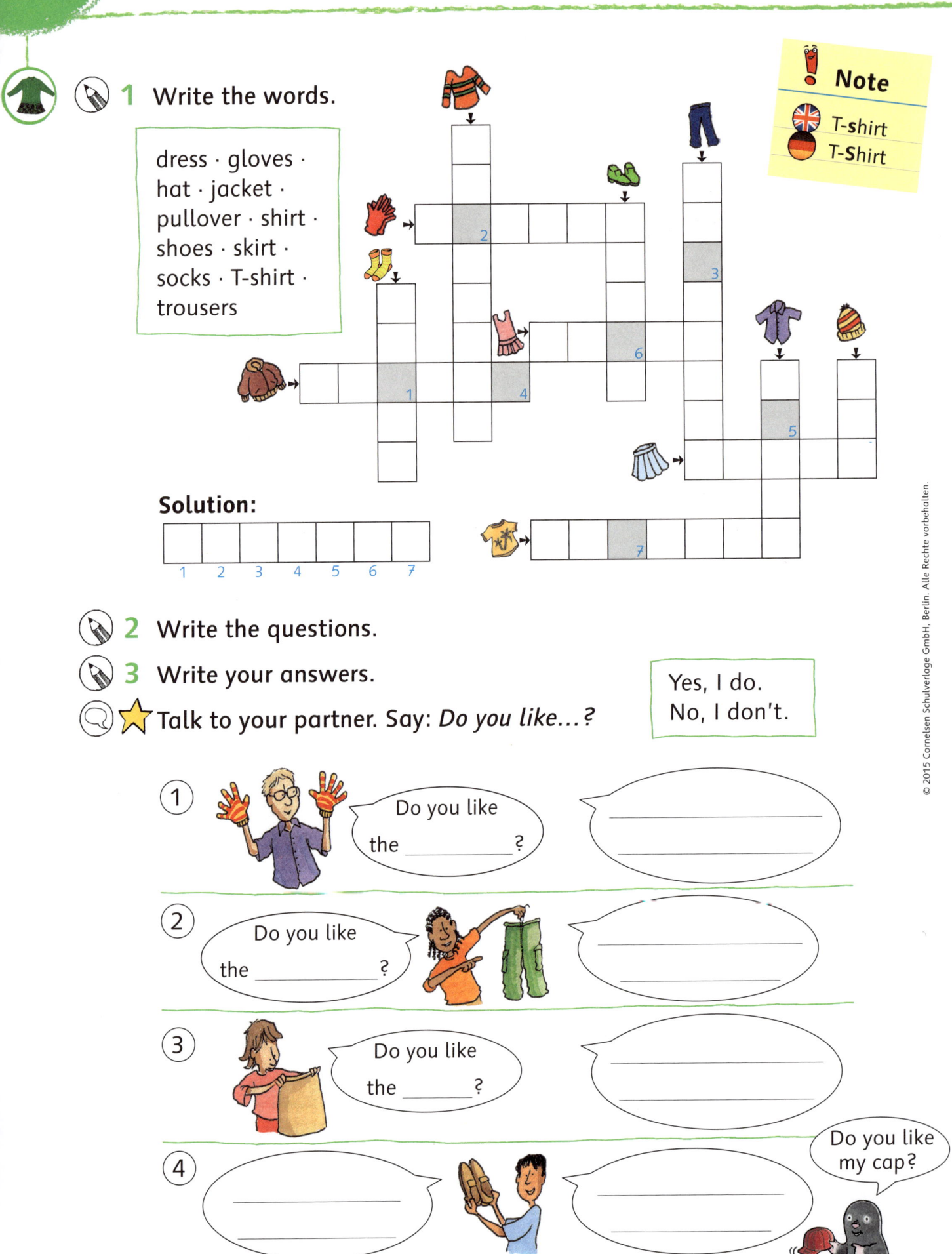

1 Write the words.

dress · gloves ·
hat · jacket ·
pullover · shirt ·
shoes · skirt ·
socks · T-shirt ·
trousers

Note
T-shirt
T-Shirt

Solution:

| | | | | | | |
|1|2|3|4|5|6|7|

2 Write the questions.

3 Write your answers.

⭐ Talk to your partner. Say: *Do you like...?*

Yes, I do.
No, I don't.

1 Do you like the _____ ?

2 Do you like the _____ ?

3 Do you like the _____ ?

4

Do you like my cap?

I'm cold.

Here's a warm hat for you.

1 Write the words.

2 Play the game with a partner.

⭐ Talk to your partner. Colour the clothes.

| · trousers | ∴ jacket | ∴· pullover | ∷ gloves | ∷· hat | ∷∷ shoes |

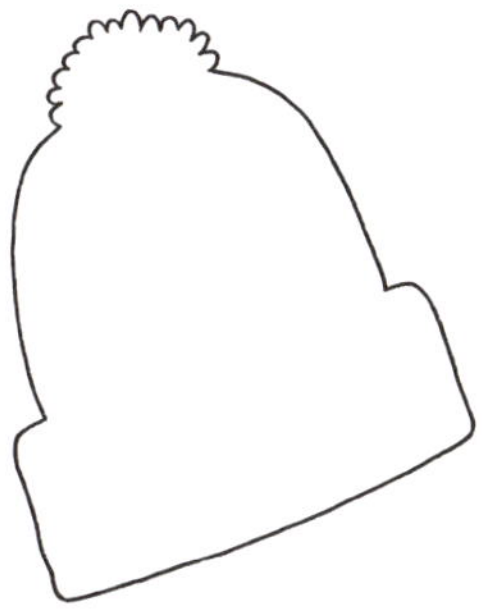

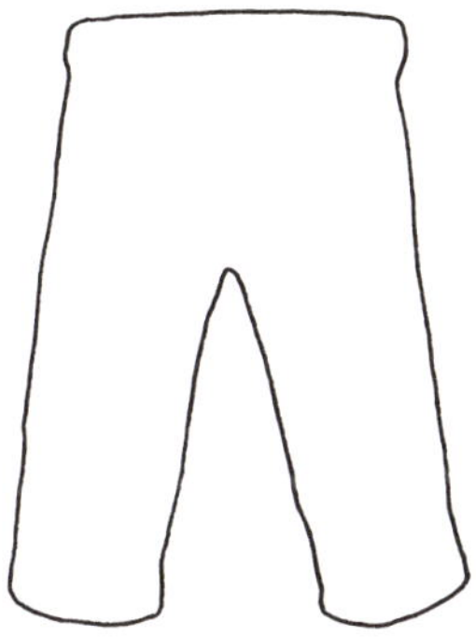

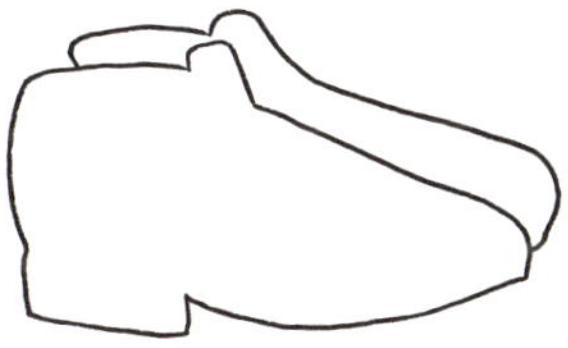

 1 What's the boy wearing? Listen and draw lines.

too small

too big

> Oh, no.
> My pullover is
> too small!

 ⭐ Talk to a partner. Write a sentence.

The _____ is too _____

 **2** Count the clothes and shoes. Write.

⭐ What's missing? Draw or write.

> dresses · hats · pullovers ·
> shirts · shoes · trousers

 There are _____

 There are _____

 There are _____

 _____

 _____

_____

Portfolio: **My favourite clothes**   The second-hand shop

I'm at   ☐ a party

   ☐ school

   ☐ _____

> **❗ Note**
>
> 🇬🇧   🇩🇪
>
> jacket – Jacke
> shoe   – Schuh
> socks – Socken

1   Write about your outfit.

I'm wearing _____

_____

_____

 ⭐ **Present your outfit in class.**

Ich fand die Aufgabe:

leicht   mittel   schwer

1

Ich habe _____ nummeriert.

Zwei Bilder sind übrig geblieben:

_____ und _____

2 Ich habe mit _____ das Lied
(Name)

Put on your clothes gesungen.

3

_____

_____

_____

_____

Ich habe geprüft, ob ich die Wörter richtig

geschrieben habe.

4 _____ und ich haben
(Name)

einander gefragt, ob uns die Kleidungsstücke

auf den Bildkarten gefallen.

5 Ich habe _____ gezeigt,
(Name)

was ich gerne anziehe, und habe vorgelesen,

was ich dazu geschrieben habe (Seite 27).

Das möchte ich noch besser können:

_____

1 Listen. What does Samir like? Tick or cross the box. (✓)(✗)

✔

Yes, I do.

✗

No, I don't.

2 Ask 2 girls and 2 boys about their hobbies.

3 Write their names. Tick their hobbies. (✓)

⭐ Ask more children.

🔍 **Note**

How many girls and boys like listening to music, …?
Make a list.

Do you like listening to music?

Yes, I do.

No, I don't.

names	listening to music	meeting friends	playing computer games	playing football	reading	watching TV	

5

Note

football – Fußball
music   – Musik

1 Read the words. Write.

⭐ Talk about your favourite hobby, music, football club, book …

listening to music · meeting friends · playing computer games · playing football · reading · watching TV

I like
_____
_____

I like
_____
_____

I like
_____

I like
_____
_____

2 Listen and number.

⭐ Make up your own dialogue.

☹ That's boring.

☺ Great idea!

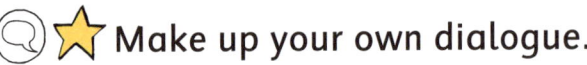
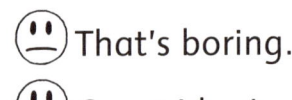

What about reading?

1 Write the names of the rooms.

2 Tell your partner what's in the rooms.
Draw pictures.

⭐ Talk about the rooms. Say: *The cat is in the ...*

🔍 Note

What else is in the rooms?
Look up the words in the
dictionary.

bathroom · bedroom · kitchen · living room

book · cat · computer · football · hamster · hat · school bag · skateboard

I can't see my room!

📖 **1** Look at the picture and read.

💬 **2** Talk about Emily's room. Say: *There's a ...*

💬 ⭐ What else is in Emily's room? Talk to a partner.

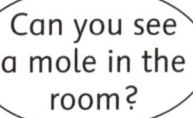

Can you see a mole in the room?

In my room, there's a chair, a table, a lamp, a wardrobe, ... I haven't got a sofa.

 3 Draw your dream room.

✏️ **4** Write.

In my dream room,

there is _____

_____

_____

_____

_____

1 What I like doing: What I don't like doing:

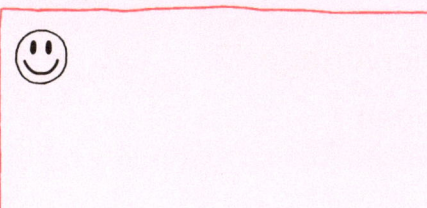   

I like _____

_____

I don't like _____

_____

My favourite hobby is _____

2 This is my room:

_____

_____

Ich fand die Aufgabe:

leicht   mittel   schwer

1 Ich habe die Abbildungen auf der Kopiervorlage 42 (Aufgabe 1 und 2) durch Linien verbunden.

Ich habe die Sätze vervollständigt. ☐

_____ und ich haben unsere
(Name)

Sätze verglichen und einander vorgelesen. ☐

2

☐ ☐ ☐ ☐ ☐ ☐

_____ und ich haben uns abwechselnd
(Name)

die Aktivitäten und Nummern dazu diktiert. ☐

3 Ich habe _____
(Name)

den Reim *Where's the cat?* aufgesagt. ☐

4 Ich habe gefragt, was _____ gerne
(Name)

macht. Ich habe gesagt, was ich mag. ☐

☐ meeting friends   ☐ watching TV   ☐ listening to music

☐ playing football   ☐ reading   ☐ playing computer games

5 Ich habe die Sätze über die Hobbys gelesen und die
Bilder dazu nummeriert (Kopiervorlage 42, Aufgabe 3). ☐

_____ und ich haben uns die Sätze vorgelesen.
(Name)

Das möchte ich noch besser können:

_____

1 Listen to your teacher. Draw lines.

2 What is it? Say or write the answer.

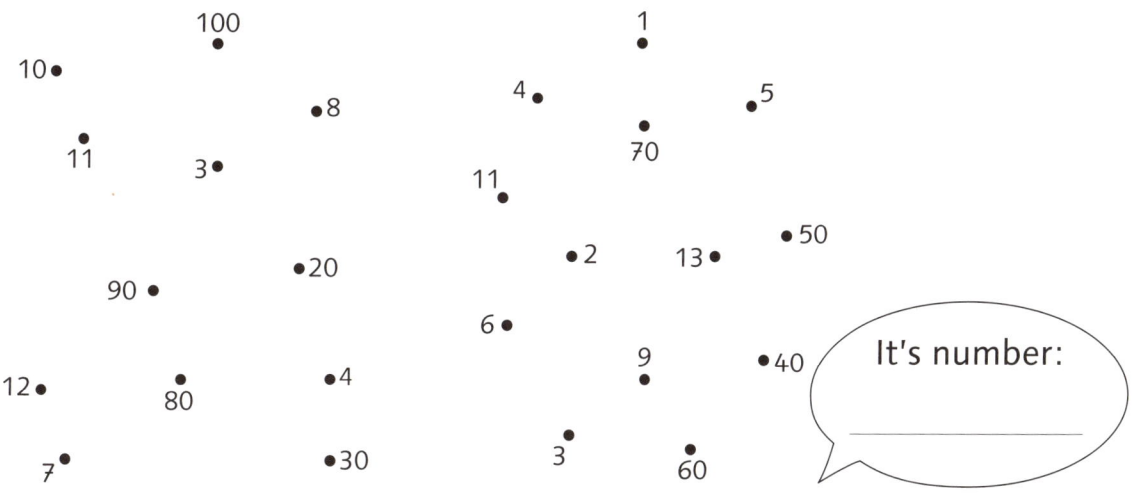

10• 100 1

•8 4• •5

11 3• 70

11•

•50

•20 •2 13•

90 • 6•

12• •4 9 •40

80 3 60 It's number:

7• •30 _____

3 Who's speaking? Listen. Circle the name.

4 What do the children like? Write.

⭐ Listen to your partner. Who is it? Find out.

I like lemon juice,
orange juice,
peach juice and
apple juice.

TIM

I like banana milk,
lemon juice,
apple _____ and
orange _____.

BEN

I like
peach _____,
apple _____,
lemon _____
and banana milk.

BOB

I like
_____ juice,
_____ juice,
_____ juice and
_____ milk.

JIM

6

1 Talk to your partner.

2 Write the words.

Play the game.

apple · banana · cherry · lemon
orange · plum · strawberry

juice · milk

Note

a banana
an orange

I'm hungry.

What about some
banana juice / a banana?

I'm thirsty.

No, thank
you.

Good
idea.

banana

banana juice

3 What do you like? Tick. (✓)

4 Talk to your partner.

I like plum
ice cream.

Do you like
apple ice cream?

Yes, I do.

No, I don't.

	apple	orange	lemon	chocolate	strawberry	vanilla	banana	cherry
My name:								
My partner's name:								

Note

In Great Britain, people pay with pounds (£) and pence (p).

1 Talk to your partner.

2 Write the prices.

How much are the apples? They're 10 p.

How much is a banana? It's 20 p.

3 Read the dialogue.

4 Number the speech bubbles. Write.

⭐ Make up your own dialogue. Act it out with a partner.

1 Hi, can I help you?
2 Yes, I'd like …
3 Anything else?
4 No, thank you.

1 Hi, can I help you?

Have you got plum ice cream?

Yes, _____ a lemon ice cream, please.

6

 1 Read.

 2 Write the dialogues.

 Act out the dialogue with a partner.

1

> I'm hot. · some ice cream

Harry: Phew, _____

Samir: What about _____?

2

> vanilla · strawberry · ice cream (2x)

Samir: A _____
for me, please.

Kate: A _____
for me, please.

3

> Here you are. · Thank you. ·
> Can I help you? · I'd like ·
> That's £ 4.40.

Where's my ice cream?

Sorry, Harry.

Woman: _____

Emily: Yes, _____
four ice creams, please.

Woman: _____

Emily: How much is it?

Woman: _____

Emily: _____

1 What's your favourite ice cream? Draw and write.

My favourite ice cream is

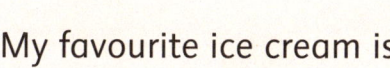

 2 What food and drinks do you like?
What don't you like? Draw and write.

Note

What else do you like?
Look up the words in the dictionary.

I like _____

_____

I don't like _____

_____

Ich fand die Aufgabe: _____

leicht mittel schwer

○ ○ ○

1 A vanilla ice cream is _____. Lemon tea is _____.

A strawberry ice cream is _____. Banana milk is _____.

A chocolate ice cream is _____. Cherry juice is _____.

_____ und ich haben die Preise verglichen.
(Name)

Wir haben uns gegenseitig die Sätze vorgelesen. ☐

2 Diese Wörter habe ich in dem Buchstabenrätsel

○ ○ ○

gefunden:

_____

_____

3 Ich habe mit _____
(Name)

○ ○ ○

das Lied *I like fruit* gesungen. ☐

4 Ich habe mit _____
(Name)

○ ○ ○

das Einkaufsgespräch gelesen und nachgespielt. ☐

5 Ich habe _____ gefragt,
(Name)

○ ○ ○

welche Eissorten er/sie mag (Seite 36). ☐

Ich habe _____ gesagt,
(Name)

welche Eissorten ich mag. ☐

Das möchte ich noch besser können:

_____

1 Read the texts.

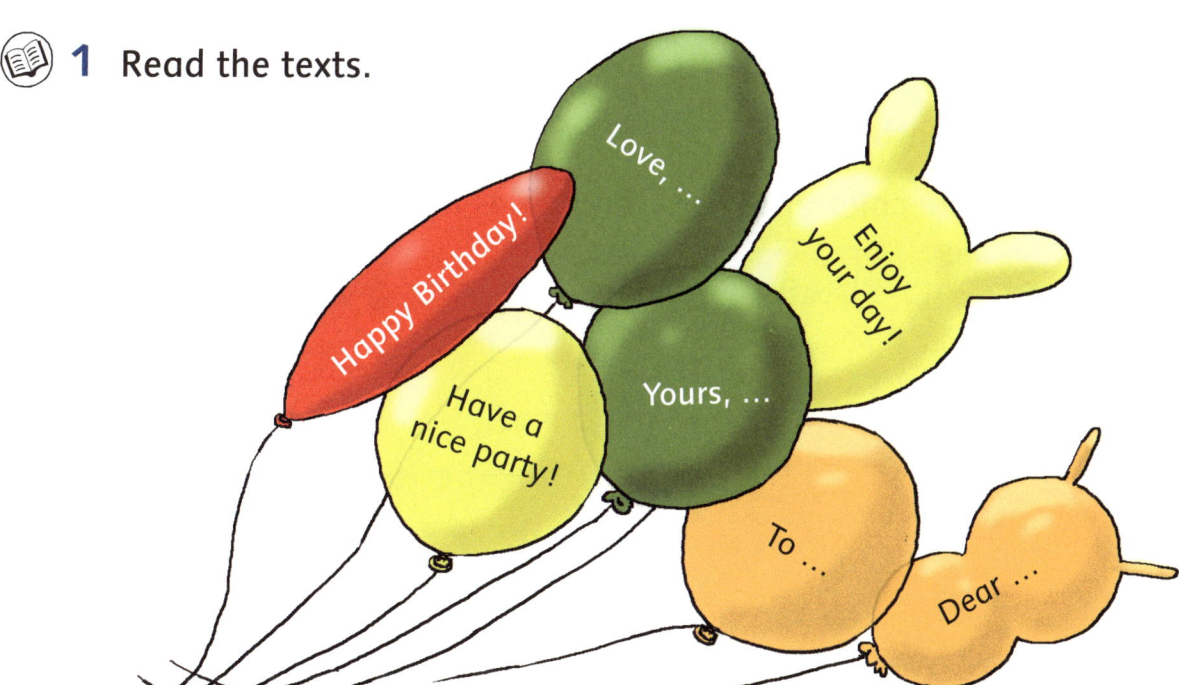

2 Write a birthday card.

Special days: **Birthday**

! Note

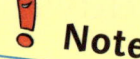 June |  Juni

Look at the other months.
Circle the differences.

 1 Read the months. Number the months.

2 Write the months.

⭐ Ask 3 or more children. Write the names in the list.

February
August
June
September
May
March
April
December
July
January
November
October

Birthdays in class _____

months	names

When
is your
birthday?

 1 Listen to the song. Look at the pictures.

 2 Read the text. Number the pictures.

 3 Write the missing words.

 Sing the song. Do the actions.

bell
chimney
hoof
reindeer
roof (2x)

①

I hear them, I hear them,

I hear them on the _____ !

②

The _____ are coming,

I hear each prancing _____ !

③

With a jingle, jingle _____

and a clop, clop, clop

④

and a clatter, clatter, clatter

at the _____ top.

⑤

I hear them, I hear them,

I hear them on the _____ !

1 What would they like for Christmas? Listen and number.

⭐ What would you like for Christmas? Talk to a partner.

2 Write sentences.

Samir would like _____

_____

_____

_____

> ❗ **Note**
>
> I would like =
> I'd like

3 Write a Christmas list.

Dear Father Christmas,

I'd like _____

_____

_____

_____ for Christmas.

From _____

Special days: **Valentine's Day**

 1 Read the poems.

2 Match the pictures to the text. Draw lines.

⭐ Circle the rhyming words.

1
I'm so happy
You are in my school
Let's go swimming
In the pool

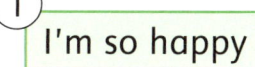

2
You are funny
You are cool
Let's have a party
After school

3
Roses are red
Violets are blue
Sugar is sweet
And so are you

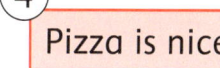

4
Pizza is nice
Spaghetti, too
Ice cream is cool
And I like you

 3 Write your own Valentine poem.

Special days: **Valentine's Day**

1 Write the words.

> cards · chocolate · February · flowers ·
> friends · heart · present · secret · Valentine

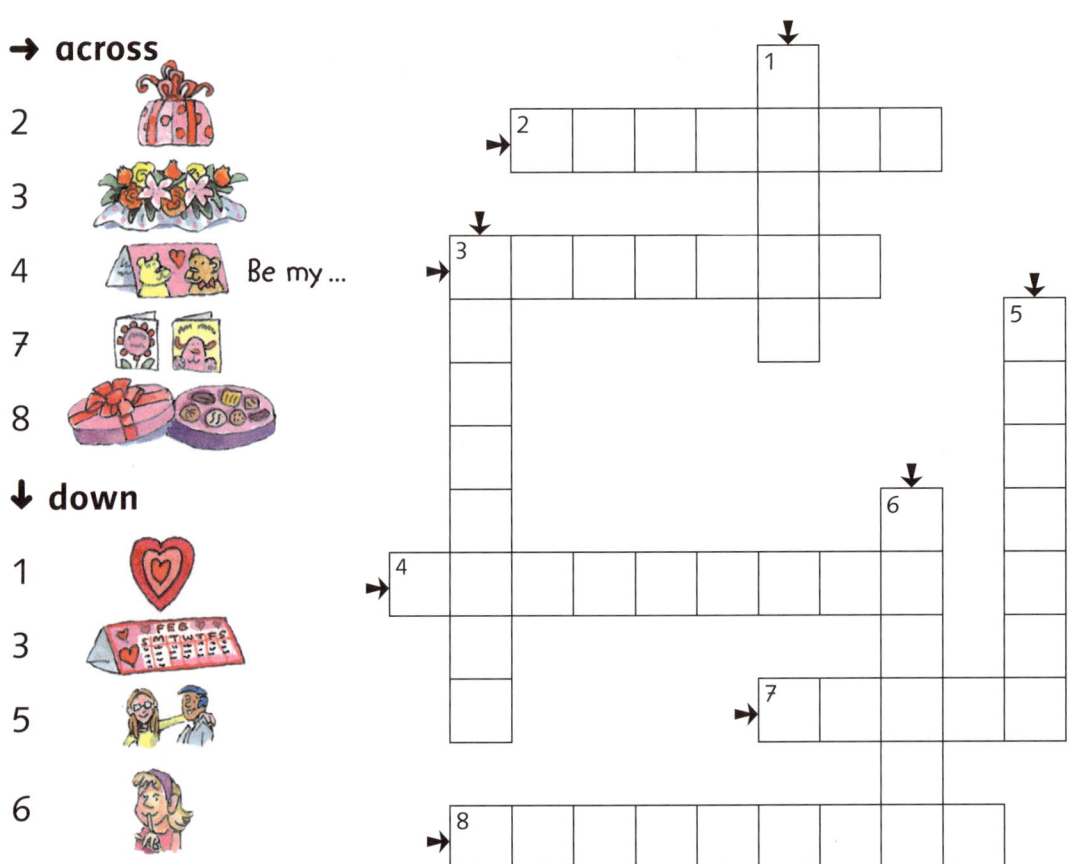

➡ **across**

2

3

4 Be my ...

7

8

⬇ **down**

1

3

5

6

2 Write Mr Mole's secret message.

Each number is a letter: (1 = A, 5 = E, 14 = N, ...)

2 5   13 25   22 1 12 5 14 20 9 14 5 !

1 Listen.

2 Draw the Easter eggs. Colour the eggs.

3 Find the words. Circle the words.

4 Write your favourite words. Talk about the words.

Special days: **Easter**

✏ **1** Draw 6 Easter eggs in your picture.

💬 **2** Talk to your partner. Draw your partner's Easter eggs in your picture.

> Where is the pink egg?

> The pink egg is …

💬 ⭐ Draw an Easter bunny in your picture. Talk to your partner.

My classroom	My partner's classroom

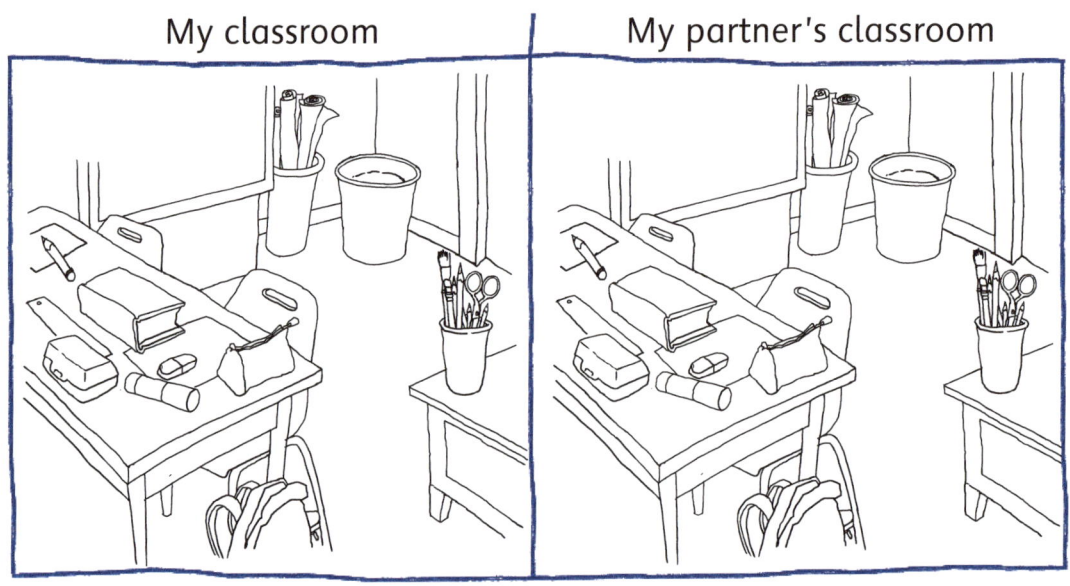

✏ **3** Draw lines and write sentences.
(Look at page 18.)

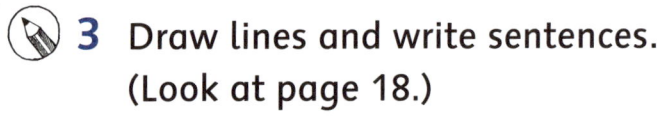

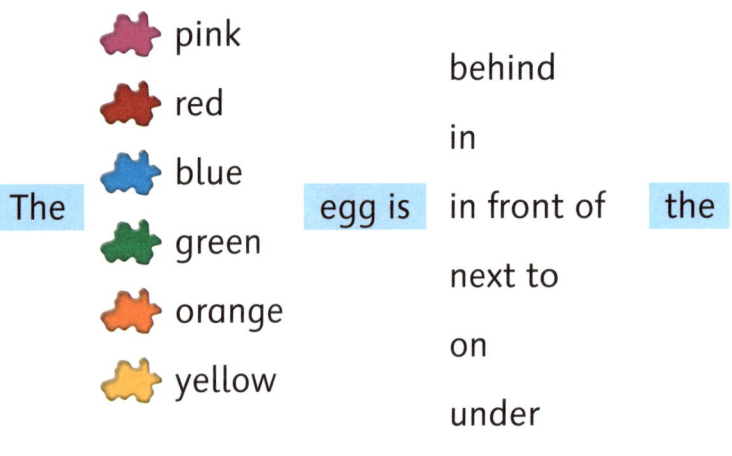

The pink egg is _____

_____

_____

Note

Choose a country.
Find out more.

1 Listen to your teacher. Point to the pictures. Where is the girl in picture 6 from?

2 Listen. Colour the flags.

☆ Listen to your partner. What country is it?

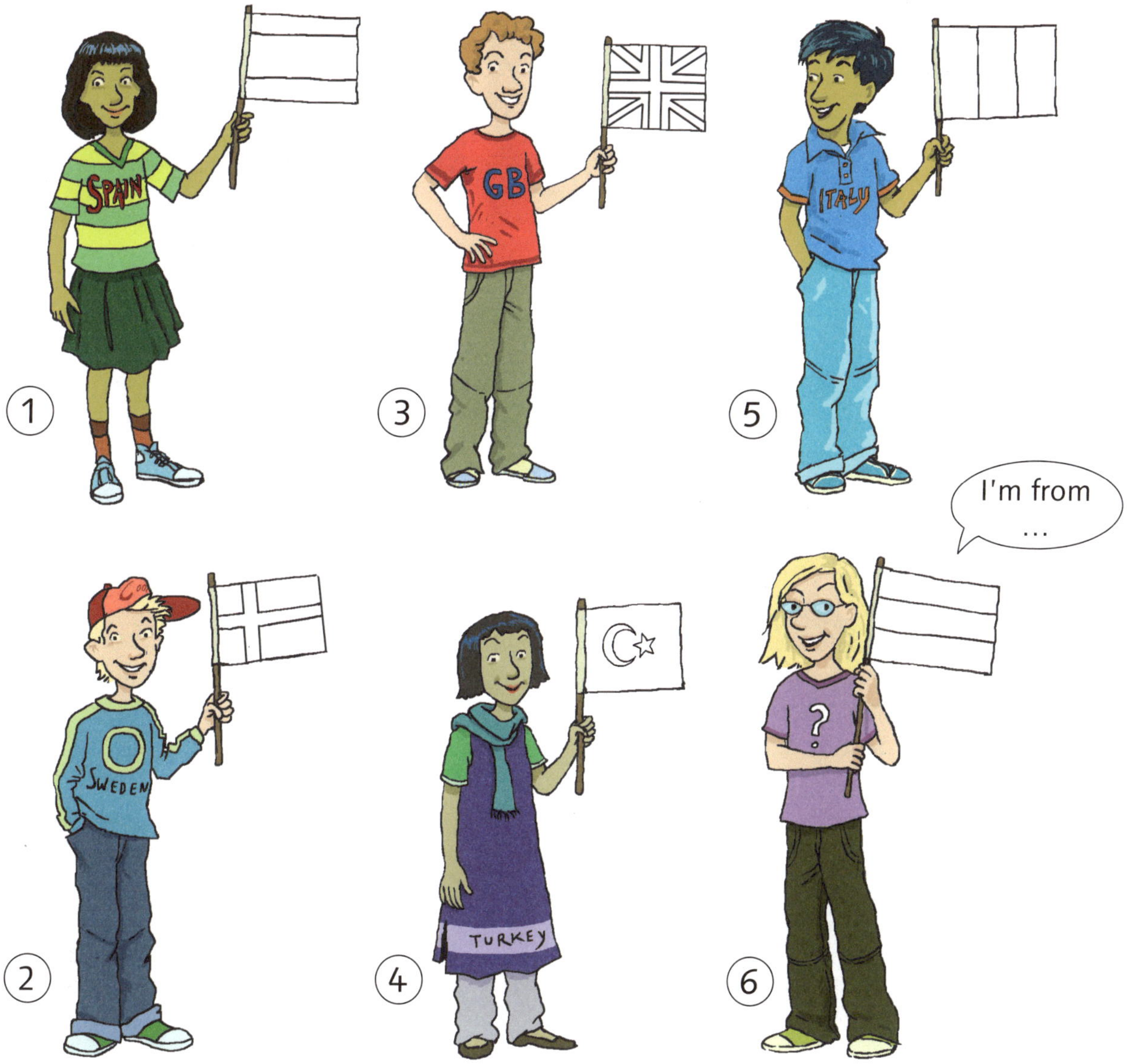
1
SPAIN
3
GB
5
ITALY
I'm from …
2
SWEDEN
4
TURKEY
6
?

3 Draw your own flag.

☆ Present your flag.

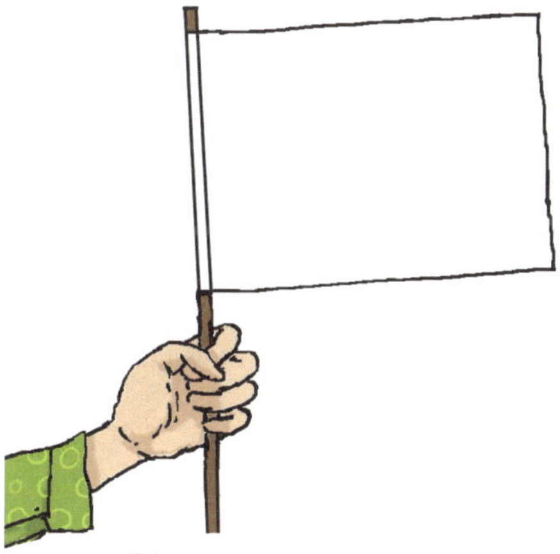

More to explore: Film **'It's a dog's life'**

1 Number the pictures.

I like dancing.

It's a black dog. Or a hamster. Or a guinea pig. Or a mouse.

I'm so happy.

Help me, I'm scared!

I can't dance, Mr Digger.

Hip, hip, hip and hop.

2 Draw the treasure.

⭐ Write.

It's a _____

Watch the film.

→ 💿 2

1 Read the sentences. Tick the right answers. (✓)

☐ The treasure is under a big tree.
☐ The treasure is on a big tree.

☐ Mr Mole is in the pencil case.
☐ Mr Mole is in the school bag.

☐ There's a cheese and ham sandwich in the lunch box.
☐ There's a cheese and tomato sandwich in the lunch box.

☐ A lollipop man is helping the children.
☐ A lollipop lady is helping the children.

2 Draw the treasure.

⭐ Write.

Watch the film.

It's a _____

More to explore: **School uniforms**

 1 Listen to your partner. Point to the clothes.

 2 Number the speech bubbles. (One speech bubble is wrong.)

1

At Swanage School all children wear red pullovers.

At Queens School boys and girls wear blue pullovers. Girls wear grey skirts.

At Blake School boys wear grey skirts and blue pullovers. All children wear green socks.

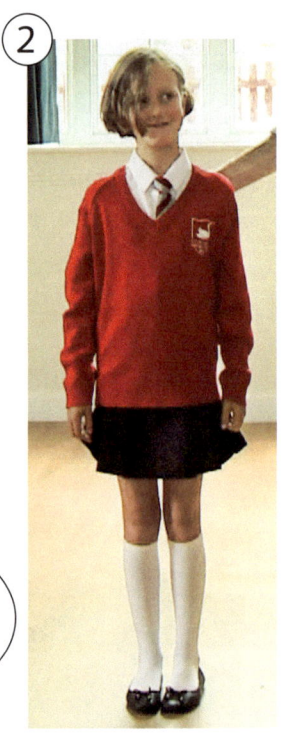
2

3 Colour the uniform. Work with a partner.

4 Tell your partner what to colour. Talk about your pictures.

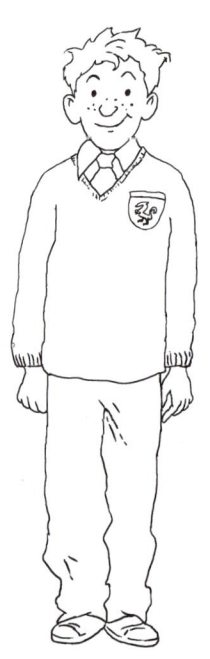

1 Listen to the rhyme. Number the text.

2 Write the rhyme. Read the rhyme with a partner.

⭐ Say the rhyme. Do the actions.

☐	Maybe so.	1 I like pink,
1	I like pink,	2 _____
☐	Yes. No.	3 _____
☐	I like blue,	4 _____
☐	I like cats.	5 _____
☐	Yes. No.	6 _____
☐	What about you?	7 _____
☐	Out you go!	8 _____

I like pink,...

3 Make up your own rhyme. Write the words.

⭐ Say your rhyme with a partner.

I like _____

_____

_____

_____

_____

_____

Words for your rhyme:

apples · black · brown · dogs · ice cream · orange · plums · purple · shampoo · TV · white

🔍 **Note**

Find more words that rhyme. Make a list.

More to explore: Film 'In the park'

 1 Read the words.

 2 Find the right order. Write the sentences. Work with a partner.

| £4.58. | Mr Digger |
| and Mr Mole | have |

_____

| is having | in the park. |
| Ben | his birthday party |

_____

| in the park. | molehills |
| 30 | There are |

_____

| very | is |
| Ice cream | cold. |

_____

 **3** Draw the treasure.

 ⭐ Write.

It's _____

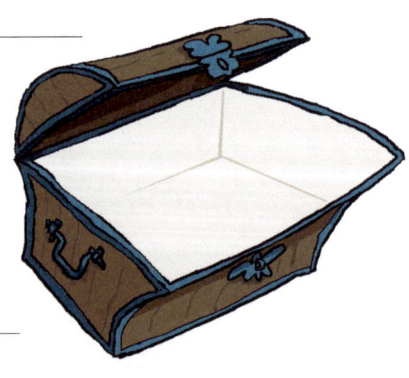

Watch the film.

→ 🔘 8

Word fields

Colours

_____ _____ _____ _____

_____ _____ _____ _____

_____ _____

Family

Colours

What colour is …?

It's …

My personal words

_____

_____

_____

_____

_____

Family

This is my family.

Have you got a brother?

No, I haven't. What about you?

I've got …

My personal words

_____

_____

_____

_____

Pets

_____ _____ _____ _____

_____ _____ _____ _____

Food

_____ _____ _____

Pets

What's your favourite pet?

My favourite pet is …

Have you got a pet?

No, I haven't.

Yes, I've got a …

My personal words

_____

_____

_____

_____

Food

What food do you like?

I like …

My personal words

_____

_____

_____

_____

School things

Clothes

School things

Can I have your …, please?

My personal words

_____

_____

_____

_____

_____

Sorry, I haven't got …

Yes, you can. Here you are.

Clothes

Do you like the shirt?

My personal words

_____

_____

_____

_____

_____

Yes, I do.

No, I don't. It's too small.

Free-time activities

_____   _____   _____

_____   _____   _____

Fruit

_____   _____   _____   _____

_____   _____   _____

Free-time activities

What are your hobbies?

My hobbies are …
What's your hobby?
Do you like …?

Yes, I like …

My personal words

_____

_____

_____

_____

_____

Fruit

Can I help you?

I'd like
an orange, please.
How much is it?

It's …
Here you are.

Thank you.

You're welcome.

My personal words

_____

_____

_____

_____

_____

Classroom talk

What my teacher says:

Stand up, please.

Sit down, please.

Look at the blackboard, please.

Come to the front, please.

Be quiet, please.

Work with a partner, please.

Open your books, please.

Listen carefully, please.

What I say:

Du möchtest wissen, was ein Wort auf Englisch heißt.

What's ... in English?

Du hast etwas nicht richtig verstanden.

Can you say it again, please?

Du möchtest jemanden um etwas bitten.

Can I have ..., please?

Du brauchst Hilfe.

Can you help me, please?

Sunshine

Lehrwerk für den früh beginnenden Englischunterricht

Activity Book 3

Erarbeitet von
Stefanie Aschkar, Konstanz; Tanja Beattie, Ebersberg; Nadine Kerler, Ulm; Caroline Schröder, München

Auf der Grundlage der Ausgabe von
Birgit Hollbrügge, Bielefeld; Ulrike Kraaz, Werther

Beratende Mitwirkung
Uwe Becker, Mannheim; Margit Butscher-Wich, Bad Abbach; Michael Duscha, Braunschweig; Renate Hafner, Blaustein; Siân Williams-Hahn, Schorndorf (englischsprachige Texte)

Verlagsredaktion
Daniela Aue (Projektleitung), Annette Burs

Illustration
Christian Bartz, Berlin; Beehive Illustration, Cirencester, England: Mike Phillips, Neil Chapman; Volker Fredrich, Hamburg; Mary Hall, Bath, England

Gesamtgestaltung
Corinna Babylon, Berlin

Technische Umsetzung
Michaela Müller für agentur corngreen, Leipzig

www.cornelsen.de

1. Auflage, 8. Druck 2023
Activity Book mit Audio CD

1. Auflage, 1. Druck 2017
Activity Book mit Audio CD und interaktiven Übungen

978-3-06-083766-3

978-3-06-081538-8

Druck: H. Heenemann, Berlin

PEFC zertifiziert
Dieses Produkt stammt aus nachhaltig bewirtschafteten Wäldern und kontrollierten Quellen.
www.pefc.de
PEFC/04-31-1156

Quellenangaben

Kapitelicons

Kind: GlowImages/Westend61; Rollschuh: Clip Dealer/Harald Fila; Hand: Fotolia/Vitalinko; Familie: GlowImage/Imagesource/Tomate: Fotolia/food pictures studio; Hund: Fotolia/grafikplusfoto; Schreibende Hand: Shutterstock/pfluegler-photo; Rucksack: Fotolia/design56; Füße: Mauritius images/Photoshot Creative/Stuart Cox; Kleid: Fotolia/Alexandra Karamyshev; Stuhl: Fotolia/Vely; Fußball: Fotolia/Andrey Kiselev; Erdbeere: Fotolia/PeJo; Geld: Fotolia/Comugnero Silvana; Kerzen: Fotolia/Ruth Black; Zweig: Your photo today. A1 pix – superbild; Muffin: Mauritius images/Alamy; Ostereier: Okapia/© Creativ Studio Heinemann/imageBROKER

Bilder

S. 50: Puppet Empire © 2015 Cornelsen Schulverlage GmbH; S. 51: Puppet Empire © 2015 Cornelsen Schulverlage GmbH; S. 52: Mauritius images/Alamy (Bild 01), Puppet Empire (Bild 02) © 2015 Cornelsen Schulverlage GmbH; S. 54: Puppet Empire © 2015 Cornelsen Schulverlage GmbH; S. 55 (v. l. n. r.): Fotolia/Alekss; Fotolia/radub85; Fotolia/magann; Fotolia/siamphoto; Fotolia/marqs; Fotolia/Les Cunliffe; Fotolia/zsaspeck; Fotolia/Tryfonov; Fotolia/verca; Fotolia/Les Cunliffe; GlowImages/Imagesource; Fotolia/tbel; S. 57: Fotolia/pwollinga; Fotolia/oxilixo; Fotolia/Irochka; Fotolia/Wojciech Kusiak; Fotolia/Vera Kuttelvaserova; Fotolia/Iosif Szasz-Fabian; Fotolia/Anatolii; Fotolia/Vera Kuttelvaserova; Shutterstock/Alexlukin; Fotolia/Sujaimages; Fotolia/Viktor Pravdica; Fotolia/PRILL Mediendesign; Fotolia/mady70; Fotolia/Marco Desscouleurs; S. 59: Fotolia/sarapulsar38; Fotolia/mrks_v; Fotolia/Karen Roach; Fotolia/M. studio; Fotolia/Dmitriy Syechin; Fotolia/Camabs; Fotolia/picsfive; Fotolia/Kotema; Fotolia/sergojpg; Fotolia/angelo19; Fotolia/smuay; Fotolia/design56; Fotolia/Africa Studio; Fotolia/ppfoto13; Fotolia/Liaurinko; Fotolia/Alexandra Karamyshev; Fotolia/Alexandra Karamyshev; Fotolia/anmalkov; Fotolia/Alexandra Karamyshev; Fotolia/ludmilafoto; S. 61: Fotolia/aletia2011; Mauritius images/Stockbroker RF; Mauritius images/Cultura; Shutterstock/Fotokostic; Mauritius images/Firstlight; Mauritius images/Cultura; Fotolia/Santiago Cornejo; Fotolia/viktoriagavril; Fotolia/Steve Cukrov; Fotolia/edu1971; Fotolia/paolofusacchia; Fotolia/Firma V; Fotolia/SashPictures

Minibildkarten

(v. l. n. r.) That's English/Toys: Cowboy: Mauritius images/Minden Pictures; Jeans: Fotolia/Yantra; Popcorn: Fotolia/ktsdesign; T-Shirt: Fotolia/ludmilafoto; Inlineskates: Fotolia/Maridav; Skateboard: Fotolia/Moiraff; Mountainbike: Fotolia/gekaskr; Fahrrad: Clip Dealer/Val Thoermer; Roller: Mauritius images/Alamy; Numbers: Mauritius images/Alamy; Mauritius images/Pixtal; Mauritius images/Alamy; Mauritius images/Pixtal; Mauritius images/Alamy; Mauritius images/Alamy; Mauritius images/Mode Images; Mauritius images/Alamy; Mauritius images/Alamy; Mauritius images/Alamy; Fotolia/William Richardson; Fotolia/Delphimages; Colours: Fotolia/Alekss; Fotolia/radub85; Fotolia/magann; Fotolia/siamphoto; Fotolia/marqs; Fotolia/Les Cunliffe; Fotolia/zsaspeck; Fotolia/Tryfonov; Fotolia/verca; Fotolia/Les Cunliffe; Family/Food: Fotolia/Alexandr Vasilyev; (Bild 02, 03, 06, 07) Fotolia/Andrev Popov; (Bild 04,05) Fotolia/lunaundmo; Fotolia/Marco Desscouleurs; Fotolia/Sujaimages; Fotolia/Viktor Pravdica, Fotolia/PRILL Mediendesign; Fotolia/mady70; Shutterstock/Alexlukin; Fotolia/pwollinga; Fotolia/oxilixo; Fotolia/Irochka; Fotolia/Wojciech Kusiak; Fotolia/Vera Kuttelvaserova; Fotolia/Iosif Szasz-Fabian; Fotolia/Anatolii; Fotolia/Vera Kuttelvaserova; School things: Fotolia/sarapulsar38; Fotolia/mrks_v; Fotolia/Karen Roach; Fotolia/M. studio; Fotolia/Dmitriy Syechin; Fotolia/Camabs; Fotolia/picsfive; Fotolia/Kotema; Fotolia/sergojp; Fotolia/angelo19; Fotolia/smuay; Fotolia/design56; Clothes: Fotolia/Africa Studio; Fotolia/ppfoto 13; Fotolia/Liaurinko; Fotolia/Alexandra; Fotolia/Alexandra; Fotolia/anmalkov; Fotolia/Alexandra; Fotolia/ludmilafoto; Fotolia/OlegDoroshin; Fotolia/Roman Sigaev; Freetime activities/Furniture: Mauritius images/Stockbroker RF; Mauritius images/Cultura; Fotolia/aletia2011; Shutterstock/Fotokostic; Mauritius images/Firstlight; Mauritius images/Cultura; Fotolia/Andrey Bandurenko; Fotolia/Vely; Fotolia/baitoey; Fotolia/HandmadePictures; Fotolia/casanowe; Fotolia/Malsveta; Fruit: Fotolia/Santiago Cornejo; Fotolia/viktoriagavril; Fotolia/Steve Cukrov; Fotolia/edu1971; Fotolia/paolofuscacchia; Fotolia/Firma V; Fotolia/SashPictures; Birthday/Christmas: Fotolia/Jenny Sturm; Fotolia/Africa Studio; Fotolia/eyetronic; Clip Dealer/Wavebreak Media LTD; Fotolia/Nik; Clip Dealer/Andres Rodriguez; Fotolia/Michael Gray; Fotolia/Phimak; Fotolia/OlegDoroshin; Fotolia/Michael Gray; Clip Dealer/Smileus; Easter/Valentine's Day: Okapia/© Creativ Studio Heinemann/imageBROKER; Fotolia/eyetronic; Clip Dealer/kostrez; Clip Dealer/Deyan Georgiev; Clip Dealer/Berislav; Clip Dealer/Cgissemann; Clip Dealer/cora mueller

Colours

Family / Food

Food / Pets

School things

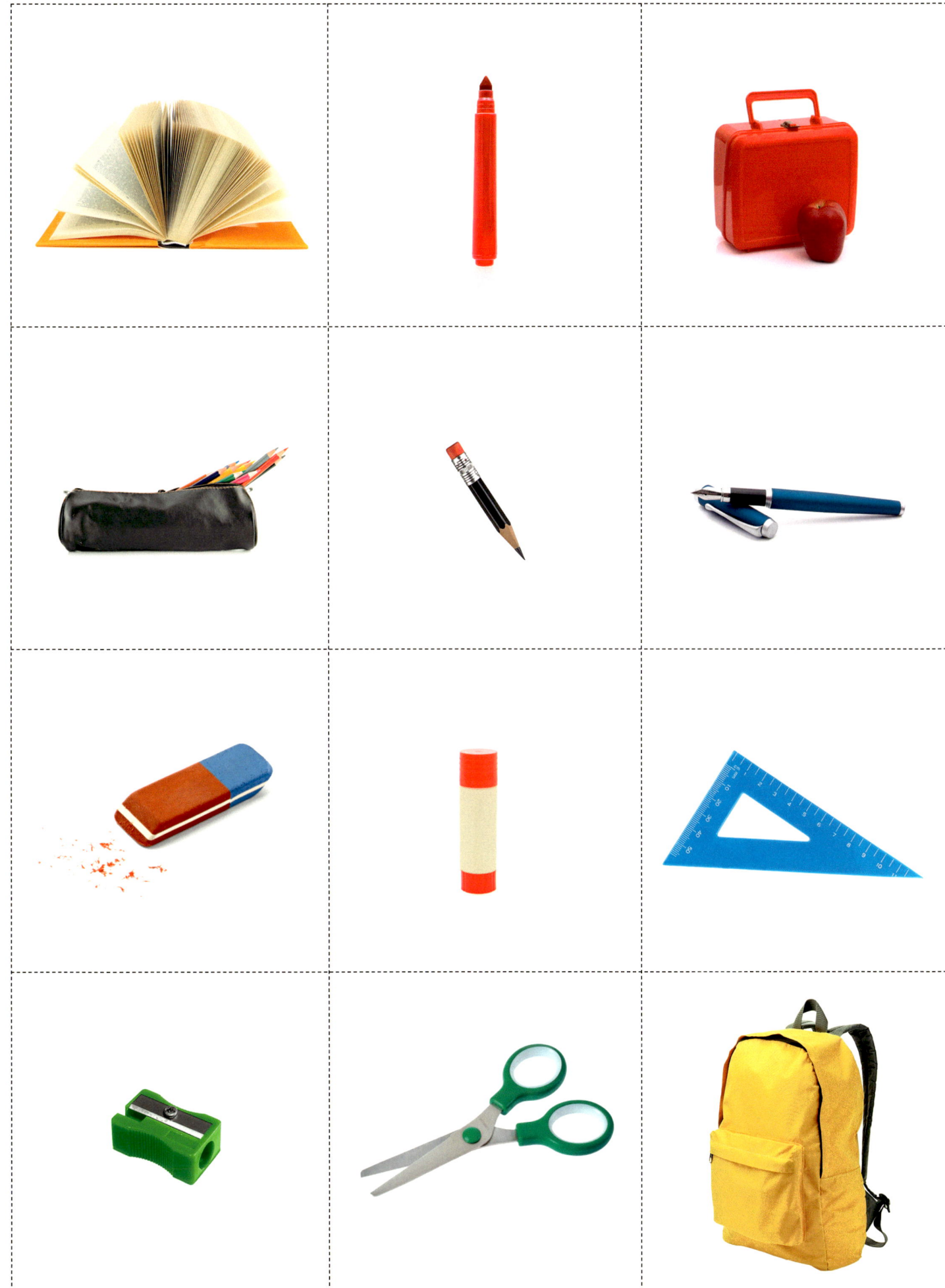

That's English	Toys	Numbers
cowboy	bike	one
jeans	in-line skates	two
popcorn	mountain bike	three
T-shirt	scooter	four
	skateboard	five
		six
		seven
		eight
		nine
		ten
		eleven
		twelve

Colours	Family	Food
black	baby	apple
blue	brother	bread
brown	father	carrot
green	grandfather	lettuce
grey	grandmother	peanuts
orange	mother	tomato
pink	sister	
red		
yellow		
white		

Pets	School things	Clothes
cat	book	dress
dog	felt tip	gloves
fish	glue stick	hat
guinea pig	lunch box	jacket
hamster	pen	pullover
mouse	pencil	shirt
rabbit	pencil case	shoes
rat	pencil sharpener	skirt
	rubber	socks
	ruler	trousers
	school bag	
	scissors	

Free-time activities	Furniture	Fruit
listening to music	bed	banana
meeting friends	chair	cherry
playing computer games	lamp	lemon
playing football	sofa	orange
reading	table	peach
watching TV	wardrobe	plum
		strawberry

Birthday	Christmas	Easter
birthday cake	Christmas cracker	Easter basket
birthday card	Christmas Day	Easter bunny
birthday present	Christmas Eve	Easter egg
candle	Christmas tree	
	stockings	
	Father Christmas	
	reindeer	

Valentine's Day		
Valentine card		
chocolate		
flower		
heart		

Clothes

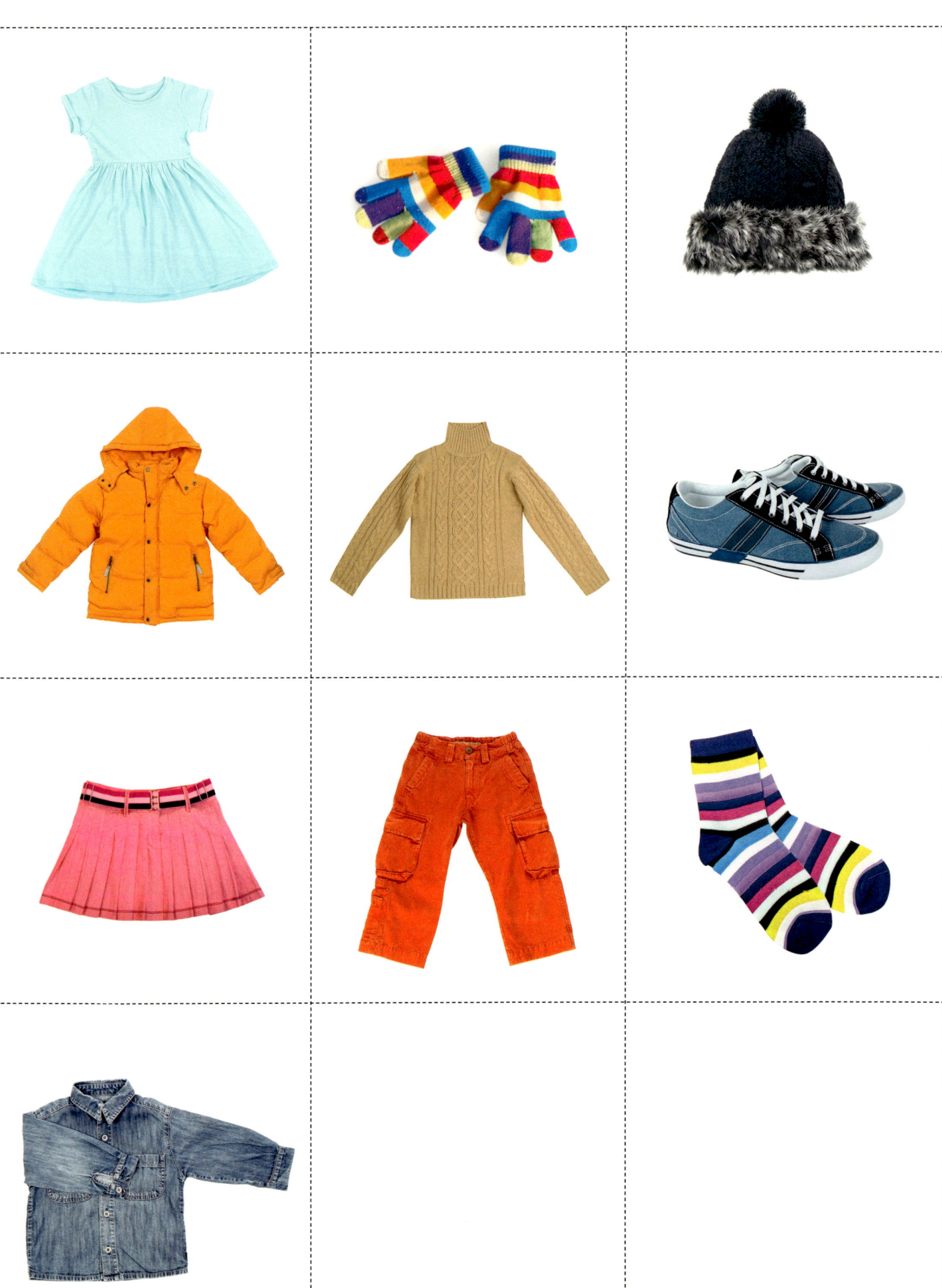

Free-time activities / Furniture

Fruit

Birthday / Christmas

Easter/Valentine's Day